The Power of the Endless Blessing

by

Miriam Hellman

The Power of the Endless Blessing

ISBN 1-891309-00-5

Published by:
Prophetic Ministries
2013 Que Street, NW,
Washington, DC 20009
Tel: (202) 265-4249; 1-800-869-5615;
Fax: (202) 265-7318
e-mail: prophmin@erols.com
www.miriamhellman.org

Other books by Miriam Hellman may be obtained from Prophetic Ministries:

Why Blood? Re-Creation and the New Age
God and the gods – Travelers from Another World
The Seer
Sealed for the Battle
The Call
Signs and Wonders
The Prosperous Soul
Offense
Ministry – A Way of Life

All Scripture quotations are taken from the Authorized King James Version of the Bible

Preface

This book does not contain all of the revelation the Holy Spirit has given concerning the anointing for finances. For further insights, I recommend our tape albums entitled ***"Miraculous Revelations and Finances" and "Financial Vision for the Future."***

Contents

Introduction

The Power of the Endless Blessing is a book of meditations designed to strengthen the spirit and soul of the believer. After reading and meditating upon these messages, one should arrive at the point where there is an ability to receive the financial blessings promised in the Word of God on a regular basis.

It is sad to observe that most of the *giving body of Christ* have only received the blessings attributed to giving. It is written, "It is more blessed to give than to receive" (Acts 20:35), but it seems that few have ever experienced with regularity the blessings of *receiving* promised to the giver.

These meditations are inspired by the Holy Spirit. I suggest that you meditate on one message every day for several days, or for a week at a time, until your spirit and soul have been engrafted with the word that will open your spirit to become a receiver of the blessings. It is my prayer that you will feed on these spiritual messages in the same way that you have learned to feed on faith food for other needs, and healing scriptures for preparing the heart to receive healing.

It is time to let your soul delight itself in fatness, and receive faith for the finances needed in the days ahead for all that God has ordained for you!

Miriam Hellman

RESURRECTION SEED

One day the Lord began to speak these words to me: "Life and death, *or* life, death and resurrection." People are always talking about life and death. The moment you're born -- until the rapture -- death is appointed to everyone.

The Lord began to speak a great revelation to me concerning the parable of the sower and the seed. We know that Jesus said that if you understand the mystery of the parable of the sower and the seed, then you can understand all mysteries. It is *the* most important parable of all the parables, because it is the key to all the mysteries of the kingdom of God.

There are many, many, many different ways this parable can be preached and taught. But the Lord spoke something fresh and vibrant into my spirit. He said, "This is the meaning of the parable of the sower and the seed. Depending upon the kind of ground the seed is planted in, it will experience either life and death, or life, death and **resurrection**."

Every seed that falls into the ground dies, but not all are resurrected. Think about that. It is a great truth. The scripture tells us that only those who are of a good and an honest heart (speaking of the ground of the heart) produce thirty, sixty, and one hundred fold.

As you plant your seed, meditate on this: That it not be seed that is just planted, but it is seed that will be resurrected -- seed that is going to bear fruit.

The scripture says that God will give seed to the sower. As you sow, you must enter into the spirit, believing for the resurrection of your seed -- not just the planting of it, but the **resurrection** of it!

COME BUY WITHOUT MONEY AND PRICE

Isaiah 55:1-3

1 *Ho, every one that thirsteth, come ye to the waters, and he that hath no money; come ye, buy, and eat; yea, come, buy wine and milk without money and without price.*

2 *Wherefore do ye spend money for that which is not bread? and your labour for that which satisfieth not? hearken diligently unto me, and eat ye that which is good, and let your soul delight itself in fatness.*

3 *Incline your ear, and come unto me: hear, and your soul shall live; and I will make an everlasting covenant with you, even the sure mercies of David.*

In the world, there's a certain type of person that wants something for nothing. Those types are never straight. There is no such thing as something for nothing. In fact, the prisons are full of people who wanted something for nothing. All their energies went into doing something that was not straight. But God has given us a tremendous, extraordinary promise in Isaiah 55 that we may buy without money.

An amazing thing happened to me while I was in New York City holding a series of meetings. My first night there, I was talking with a group of people before the meeting began. I casually mentioned to a gentleman sitting to my right that I was going shopping the next day for fabric to make banners for our camp meeting. I told him I knew there was no place in the world like New York City where so many special kinds of fabric could be found, so I was going to go and buy certain kinds of material needed for our banners while I was in town.

I didn't have very much money. In fact, all I had was $50.00, which isn't enough to do the job by any means. But I was believing that God was going to direct me to supernatural bargains and extraordinary remnants, and that He would provide.

So, as I casually mentioned what I was going to do, the man said, "By all means do not go shopping tomorrow. Come to me first. I have a warehouse filled with fabric. I fireproof materials that go into hotels and public buildings. I have lots of leftover fabric, so please, come and help yourself."

The next day we went to the warehouse, and I came home with a whole trunkload of fabrics far beyond what we were looking for. I also received a great bonus. In my living room, I have furniture I really enjoy. I had noticed it really looked worn and needed to be reupholstered, but I thought I would never find this particular pattern and color of velvet, since it had come from Israel. But there in that warehouse in New York was an enormous bolt of that very fabric!

The Lord supplied exceedingly, abundantly, above and beyond what we needed. A lady who was with us in New York estimated that we came home with $15,000 worth of material!

Many times when you have no money, you take leftovers -- things no one else wants -- others' rejects. You might get it without money, but it wouldn't be just that perfect thing. But God is able to do things in extraordinary ways if our hearts are right. We may buy without money and ***without price***.

I praise the Lord that what we received was so extraordinary -- perfect and beautiful. There is no price range too high for the Holy Spirit!

BELIEVE AND RECEIVE

When you give, ***believe*** that God is going to bless you in your giving. You play a very important and instrumental role in everything that you do in your spiritual and natural life. Don't just give as though you are fulfilling a duty, but give ***believing*** that you shall receive.

THE REALM OF CONTINUOUS MIRACLES

As we prepare to give, we want to prepare our hearts to believe that God is going to do abundantly.

Some time ago, the Lord gave me a message concerning living in a continuous miracle. Ever since I preached that message, I having been living in a continuous miracle twenty-four hours a day. This is the only place to live! We have to leave the beggarly elements and lower levels behind and go on into the realm of glory.

The place to begin is with your offerings. You have to begin to believe that your offerings are working in a continuous way. My tithes and offerings are working in a continuous way for me. If they are working for me, your tithes and offerings can also be working for you.

I am believing that what is in my heart is going to be in your heart. When you have this revelation in your heart, you, too, are going to live in that realm of continuous miracles!

THE GOOD AND HONEST HEART

There is a profound message in the parable of the sower and the seed. It tells the story of three different groups of people. There is only one group in that parable that ever produces, and that group produces thirty, sixty, and one hundred fold. That group has a good and an honest heart. That means honest with God and honest with your fellow man in all things. These are the people who produce. The other categories never ever produce. It is because of the way they respond to the things that happen to them in life. Their response is a worldly response, and it doesn't produce.

The Lord showed me that there is life and death, or there is life, death and **resurrection**. Many of us have given much to the Lord, but we have seen little in return. We have truly planted the seed, but every seed planted has fallen to the earth and died.

The Lord began to impress upon me that every single penny I give should be perceived and believed to be resurrection seed -- not merely as a giving and a planting, because not all that is planted is resurrected.

The Lord also spoke to me to tithe as I want my income to be. He said not to tithe on what it actually is, but to tithe based on what it should be.

If you can catch this, you can also have it!

SACRIFICE

As we've given to the gospel, I believe we've never understood how precious sacrifice is to the Lord.

The threshing floor where the angel of destruction stood is where the temple was built in Jerusalem. David bought this site with a sacrificial offering and turned the place of destruction into the place of the holy of holies. He said, "I will verily buy it for the full price: for I will not take that which is thine for the Lord, nor offer burnt offerings without cost" (I Chronicles 21:24).

I pray that each and every one of us will understand and comprehend the length, the breadth, the depth and the height of the meaning of sacrifice.

BETWEEN A ROCK AND A HARD PLACE

Not long ago, the Lord spoke to me for an entire week about Jacob lying down with a stone for his pillow. Have you ever noticed all those people who had stones for pillows in the Old Testament? Now, just ask yourself: If you put in a long, hard day trekking across the desert, would you put a stone under your head? I had never understood this, but one night it became clear as the Lord spoke to me.

Jacob was in fear, running from his brother. He had many problems in his life, and he was literally between a rock and a hard place. While he was between a rock and a hard place, (the rock being his head and the hard place, the ground in this predicament), all of a sudden he has a great vision. He sees the gate to heaven, and heaven is opened to him in the midst of this hard place.

Jacob was spiritually and circumstantially in a very difficult place in his life. In the natural, he was **literally** between a rock and a hard place. This place in his life was where the gate of heaven opened up to him. This is also true in our lives -- when we are between a rock and a hard place, oftentimes this is where the gateway to heaven is revealed to us. It was revealed to Jacob in such a place, and when that gate was revealed, he got up from his sleep and poured oil upon the rock. He made a vow unto the Lord and said, "Lord, if you will be with me forever, and if you will take care of me and feed me and clothe me, I'm yours. I will stay with you forever, if you will be with me."

We all go through difficult situations from time to time -- and this is not limited to problems in the area of finances. Jacob did not have financial difficulties at this time of crisis in his life. He had problems within his family and many circumstances that were contrary. In times of difficulty, if we will pour out unto the Lord an offering, the gate of heaven will also be opened unto us. That is exactly what Jacob did, and he went from that place of great distress and crisis to his unlimited inheritance in God. It was the turning point in his life when he was between a rock and a hard place.

BEING AN OPEN CHANNEL FOR GOD'S BLESSINGS

About five or six people have given $100.00 to this ministry and have received the one hundred fold return -- $10,000.00. (There are also others who have given more and gotten even greater rewards.) In each one of these instances, I think the longest period of time that elapsed was six weeks from the time the person gave the offering until they received the one hundred fold return.

The first time this happened, I was so excited that someone had received $10,000.00! It was a miracle how the person received it. When I told my pastor, he said, "You had better go to that person immediately and tell them to tithe to you right away from that, or they are going to lose their blessings." When I heard his remark, a reaction went off inside of me. Call it spiritual pride, lack of nerve or whatever, I just could not go to that person and tell them they had to tithe to me. I had never heard anyone say that, and I thought, "Oh, how crass to go and say such a thing." I just couldn't do it.

I told my pastor, "Oh, I couldn't go and say that." He replied, "I am telling you that if you do not tell this person, and if they don't do it, they are: number one, robbing God; number two, robbing themselves; and three, robbing your ministry. This is the ordained way in which you live in a continuous flow of financial blessings. The blessing should come back to the ministry through which the blessing originally came. If you receive from one ministry and then put your finances into another ministry where you are not receiving as much, you are working against your spiritual blessings, and you are going to have leanness."

Well, I just couldn't go to the person and tell them they should tithe ten percent from that $10,000.00. I just *couldn't* bring myself to do it. Every Sunday, my pastor would ask me, "Did you speak to that person?," and my response was always the same, "No. I didn't."

About two months went by. I was ministering one day, and the person who had received the $10,000.00 was there, talking with a group of people. I overheard the person say they hadn't known what to do when they received the $10,000.00. They knew of a ministry which had never gotten off the ground that was always in debt and had lots of problems. This person decided to help this ministry out -- they gave the tithe from the $10,000.00 to that ministry.

The recipient of the $10,000.00 contacted me two years later. They said, "We've had nothing but leanness ever since that $10,000.00 came in." I said, "You must forgive me. My pastor repeatedly told me to go to you and tell you the tithe from the $10,000.00 should have gone to my ministry. He said if it went elsewhere, leanness would result. I'm sorry, but I just didn't have the courage to say this." They said, "We wish you had."

In subsequent matters, I *have* had the courage -- I just hadn't understood the principle involved. But after my pastor explained it, I heard other ministers say the same thing -- that we are to give where we are being blessed. They must have been saying this all along, however hearing without understanding avails little.

When we follow God's plan, He will use us to be a continual open channel for His blessings.

ETERNAL BLESSINGS FROM THE ETERNAL GOD

Tithes and offerings are not given unto men, but they are given unto the Lord Jesus Christ who is our high priest in heaven. We give unto the Lord -- not unto man. We give unto the Lord who lives and abides forever.

As the Word of God states, in the loins of Abraham were Isaac and Jacob, who paid tithes through their father. As we pay our tithes and offerings from our hearts, we are blessing the children the Lord has given us -- born and unborn -- for they come under our roof and under the heritage and blessings given us by the Lord.

INHERITANCE BY PROMISE

The 12th chapter of Genesis describes the blessings of Abraham. The blessings of Abraham are ours -- *we* are the sons and daughters of Abraham. This means that we partake of the same inheritance, which is an inheritance before the law. It is an inheritance by *promise.* All of our blessings are by promise -- the blessings of the New Testament are by promise.

We receive our blessings the same way that Abraham received his. He did not receive his blessings by law -- he received his blessings by *promise.* We are to be partakers of this promise, and this promise covers more than just our finances.

Genesis 12:1-3

1 *Now the Lord had said unto Abram, Get thee out of thy country, and from thy kindred, and from thy father's house, unto a land that I will shew thee:*

2 *And I will make of thee a great nation, and I will bless thee, and make thy name great; and thou shalt be a blessing:*

3 *And I will bless them that bless thee, and curse him that curseth thee: and in thee shall all families of the earth be blessed.*

Verse 1 tells us the beginning of Abraham's blessings was to get out of all attachments to family. Not that you are to turn your back on your family, but when family is more important than the Word of God, your blessings will not be forthcoming.

We are to be partakers of the land of plenty. We are to be the partakers of the promised land! The promised land has promised benefits in it. You can appropriate "and I will make thy name great" for yourself. God wants to make your name great. That means that when your name is mentioned, people are immediately going to think, "Oh, what great things God does for you."

Your name is very important. God wants to use your name so that when your name is spoken, you are going to be known as one who is a possessor of the promises. That's what it means. It is not like having your name in the newspaper or being known in Hollywood. You need to get this in your spirit: God wants *your* name to be spoken about. He wants *your* name to be associated with His blessings. Then you shall be a blessing.

You, yourself, are going to be a blessing to others. This is the reason for being blessed -- so you can be a blessing to others. Those who bless you are going to be blessed by God. However they bless you, they will be blessed -- whether it's financially or some other way. They are going to be blessed because they blessed you.

Over the years, we have had a house full of people from all around the world. Before we were saved, we used to call our house a hotel. Then we actually ran a hotel for seven years and we had more people. Now I have letters coming into my office every day from people who are coming to Washington, so we still have a hotel, so to speak.

We have always had our door open. Sometimes it hasn't been convenient, and sometimes it is a lot of extra work, but we've enjoyed it because hospitality is a gift through which the Holy Spirit works. The Bible tells us to be careful to entertain strangers, for you may entertain angels unaware. Because of our open door, wherever I have gone in the world I have never lacked for a wonderful place to stay.

We've also given people rides to church for years. We were *the* official Christian taxi in Jerusalem. Our car went daily to Hadassah Hospital -- we took neighbors, we took soldiers. We used our car in every way possible to be a blessing to others. As a result, I've never lacked a ride anyplace, anywhere. I've gone places unexpectedly, and people have just come and given me the keys to their car or paid my airplane ticket.

As you bless, people will also bless you. The people who bless you will also be blessed, and you should believe that for them. That is part of *your* responsibility -- not just the minister who stands up and prays over the offering -- but *you* pray and believe that those who bless you will also be blessed.

Anyone who comes against you will be dealt with by God, Himself. That is also part of the blessing. I've seen it happen over and over again. You don't have to do anything -- it's an automatic part of the blessing that those who come against you, God will come against. You don't have to be worried about it -- God will just take care of it.

In the Bible, there is no record that anyone ever prayed against those doing evil to them. David always asked God to bless his enemies, and look what happened to him. They got the curse, and David got the blessing!

We should also seek to be a blessing to all the families of the earth. In Psalm 2:8, we read, "Ask of me, and I will give thee the nations for thine inheritance, and the uttermost parts of the earth for thy possession." God wants us to be a blessing to all the families of the earth, so it is important to give to those ministers who are anointed of God to reach the nations.

As we give, we need to believe that we also will receive the blessings of Abraham. Giving is a blessing, and as we bless, we become partakers of the sevenfold blessings of Abraham.

THE LAW OF RELEASE

There are many more types of giving other than financial giving. There are many aspects of giving, and all areas of lack are taken care of by giving. According to the law of release -- not just the law of the Old Testament release, but the law of the spirit of life in Christ Jesus -- there are three areas that involve release. They are: giving, thanksgiving, and forgiving. All three involve *giving*! If we give thanksgiving, we get the release. If we are forgiving, then our heavenly Father forgives us, also.

Thanksgiving, forgiving, and giving are the means to all the releases in life!

HOLY GHOST GIVING

In the fifth chapter of the Book of Acts, we read a terrifying account of a couple, Ananias and Sapphira. No one likes to hear about them, but I don't mind hearing about them. It doesn't bother me. I'm not guilty!

When the early church began, when the fire of Pentecost fell, and the miracle power of God spilled out of the building and into the streets, there was revival in the hearts of the people. The zeal of God had consumed them, and they were as a burning fire! As they went out, miracle after miracle after miracle occurred. In one day, thousands of people were saved and filled with the Holy Ghost. Glory was everywhere and everyone was prospering.

The church began in the power and demonstration of the Holy Ghost, and *prosperity abounded*. The Bible does not speak about people who owned a piece of property -- they owned proper*ties*. They were land barons, and their prosperity was great. They began to sell their properties, putting the proceeds at the feet of the apostles. One of the many people who sold his property at the direction of the Holy Spirit was Barnabus, who became an apostle.

Ananias and Sapphira also owned a piece of property. The Lord showed me they prayed about this property and asked what to do with it. He told them to sell it, so they did. I believe they also asked the Lord what they should do with the proceeds, and I think the Lord told them to give it all. But when it came time for the giving, they didn't give it all, to which Peter said, "Whiles it remained, was it not thine own? and after it was sold, was it not in thine own power? why hast thou conceived this thing in thine heart? thou hast not lied unto men, but unto God" (Acts 5:4). No one made them do anything. No one told them they had to give anything.

God revealed to me what it meant that these people had lied to Him. He showed me that they didn't decide of their own will what they were going to give. They had asked the Lord what to give, but did not do what the Lord told them. It was a matter of their own free will to give whatever they wanted. Even God didn't care if they wanted to give a free will offering. The lying to the Holy Ghost came when they asked the Lord what to give; the Lord told them what to give, but they disobeyed what the Lord told them to give.

If we don't ask the Lord, but just proceed with our own idea of what we're going to do, then we've lied to ourselves. But, if we've asked the Lord, the Lord is not going to put us in debt. The Lord is never going to tell you to write a check that is going to bounce. The Lord is never going to rob from your inheritance or your family. The Lord may, at times, tell you to do something unusual, but if you are really living the life that is provided in the Holy Ghost, you are only going to get ten times more in return.

Peter, by the demonstration of the Holy Spirit, declared the condition of the heart of Ananias and Sapphira. We know that they both lied and dropped dead. The spirit of truth will expose lies. After that, fear came upon everyone, but there was a great power and demonstration of the spirit of truth in the church. The spirit of truth was in such demonstration from the time this couple was judged that miracles greatly abounded. People were even brought into the street for Peter's shadow to pass over them and be healed. There was such a demonstration of glory, power, deliverance and help for everyone that the authorities became upset -- the devil was mad.

Peter was imprisoned, "But the angel of the Lord by night opened the prison doors, and brought them forth, and said, Go, stand and speak in the temple to the people all the words of this life" (Acts 5:19, 20). He was out preaching the word before the authorities even knew he was gone from the prison.

We are no longer to speak the words of death. We are no longer to live a lie. Don't live any lie in the financial area. Don't lie to yourself, and especially don't lie to the Holy Ghost.

God wants to bless us. Look what happened to Barnabus -- he became an apostle. He became a co-worker with Paul. He became mighty and eloquent in God because he didn't lie to the Holy Ghost.

Barnabus sowed into his own ministry -- not because he gave a piece of property, but because he obeyed the

Holy Ghost. Let us also purpose in our hearts to always give as the Holy Ghost directs.

THE PROPHET'S REWARD

Matthew 10:40-42

40 *He that receiveth you receiveth me, and he that receiveth me receiveth him that sent me.*

41 *He that receiveth a prophet in the name of a prophet shall receive a prophet's reward; and he that receiveth a righteous man in the name of a righteous man shall receive a righteous man's reward.*

42 *And whosoever shall give to drink unto one of these little ones a cup of cold water only in the name of a disciple, verily I say unto you, he shall in no wise lose his reward.*

These verses are speaking about the receiving of rewards. To make it very simple, we're talking about receiving Jesus. As we receive Jesus, we receive a reward -- we receive the reward of redemption -- we receive the reward of eternal life. But more important, we receive the person of Jesus and thereby receive the love of Jesus, the friendship of Jesus, the comfort, the consolation of Jesus and the healing of Jesus.

Verse 41 speaks about receiving the prophet's reward. Rewards have to do with what you have sown into. Whatsoever you sow, so shall you reap. Everything is governed by the laws of sowing and reaping. That is established beginning in Genesis, ending in Revelation. We all understand that what a man sows is what a man reaps.

Jesus speaks about whosoever receives a prophet in the name of a prophet receives a prophet's reward. Then He talks about a righteous man's reward, followed by giving a cup of cold water in the name of a disciple, and a disciple's reward. So we see there are different categories of rewards.

There may be many things we do for the people out on the street and for the body of Christ at large, and for that we receive the disciple's reward, but the highest reward is the prophet's reward. I'm not talking about the highest and greatest thing that God can give to you, but there are rewards involved with receiving the prophet and caring for the prophet.

In the Bible, we see one case where a woman observed that the prophet passed through her town. She told her husband it would be nice if they put an addition onto their house and make a room where the prophet could stay. They not only provided a room, but they provided a bed, a stool, a table and a light, so that he would have a full provision.

As the prophet began to receive from the woman, he sought a way to bless her. He found out that she did not have a child, so he pronounced the blessing of a child upon her. His word came to pass and the child was born. As time went on the child died, but that woman went right back for her prophet's reward -- she received the resurrection of a son!

People in the Bible who had no teaching, but had it in their heart, saw what they were sowing into. They didn't do it for rewards, but they saw what they were sowing into. Not only did they have immediate blessing, *but they had the blessing when they needed the blessing*. That's also part of the prophet's reward, that when you need it, it shall be there.

GIVING BRINGS A RELEASE

There are many opinions about offerings, but God isn't interested in the opinions of men. He is only interested in His own opinions.

Mark 12:41-44

41 *And Jesus sat over against the treasury, and beheld how the people cast money into the treasury: and many that were rich cast in much.*

42 *And there came a certain poor widow, and she threw in two mites, which make a farthing.*

43 *And he called unto him his disciples, and saith unto them, Verily I say unto you, That this poor widow hath cast more in, than all they which have cast into the treasury:*

44 *For they all did cast in of their abundance; but she of her want did cast in all that she had, even all her living.*

I have learned that we cannot force God into a situation in which He's going to respond on the basis of our giving. I think most people have already figured that out. It just doesn't work that way. But there is a truth about the giving of all, and the Bible does preach a sacrificial giving.

Only twice have we announced any needs of the ministry. One night we mentioned we needed a typewriter. A lady came up after the meeting and said she didn't know anything about the ministry or why she had come, but that the Lord had been dealing with her all night long. She said that she had needed a typewriter and someone had just given her one, but she was going to give my ministry that typewriter. The only stipulation was that I would have to go to her house to pick it up. I told her if she needed it, I certainly didn't want to take it from her, but she insisted that I was to have the typewriter.

At the time she gave the typewriter, this woman was going through a very hard time. She had nothing, and she literally gave all. Just weeks after giving the typewriter, tremendous financial blessings came her way, and every area of her life dramatically turned around.

BELIEVERS ARE RECEIVERS!

All the promises of God come out of the riches in glory in Christ Jesus, which is in the realm of the Spirit.

Acts 10:1-4

1 *There was a certain man in Caesarea called Cornelius, a centurion of the band called the Italian band,*

2 *A devout man, and one that feared God with all his house, which gave much alms to the people, and prayed to God alway.*

3 *He saw in a vision evidently about the ninth hour of the day an angel of God coming in to him, and saying unto him, Cornelius.*

4 *And when he looked on him, he was afraid, and said, What is it, Lord? and he said unto him, Thy prayers are come up for a memorial before God.*

God does watch the gift and the giver. There will come a time when the memorial is going to be a blessing that is going to be poured out.

There are those that are very open to receive, and then there are those who are so closed. We need to think of ourselves from this day forward as ***receivers***.

ETERNAL PURPOSES OF GOD

There are about five questions that ninety percent of the believing church world always has. One of them is: Where do you give your tithes and offerings?

Jesus told the Pharisees that they taught for doctrines the traditions of men. Many times we have lost, and have been robbed and stolen from in the area of receiving, because we have been taught the traditions of men rather than what the Word of God says in that area.

Churches and ministries say different things, but this is the message right from the Bible, and it is a powerful, powerful message: Everything connected with the power of the endless blessing has to do with the priesthood. When it comes to giving, we have to search our hearts and give to the priest -- that is, to Jesus.

I'd like to share something that has happened in my own life concerning giving. I am happy to say that I am a big giver, and that I give under the direction of the Holy Spirit. Lately the Lord has been causing me to increase my giving -- I've been giving a lot more than usual.

The Lord recently spoke something to me that He wanted me to do. This is hard for me to say, but I was terrified at the thought of it. To me, it was an awfully big assignment in God. I didn't know if I had the wisdom to do it. But the Lord told me He wouldn't ask anyone to do something who didn't already have adequate wisdom, or know how to appropriate the amount of wisdom necessary to complete the task.

Because of the awesomeness of the task, I had shoved it to the back of my mind. After a week went by, God spoke to me and said, "You *will* do this." He said, "You will go at my command and do this." I never even considered the money that would be needed to accomplish the assignment. The task was so awesome that I never thought beyond the task itself.

Five months earlier, I had received a prophecy that the Lord was going to send me on errands for Him - that these things would be too difficult for many people, but for me they would be easy, because it would be the Lord. The Lord also said that when He sent me, He would put the finances in my hands. Several weeks after this word was given to me, someone came up to me and said, "Someone tried to reach you this morning because God spoke to them to give you a certain amount of money." I said, "They did?" But I was so consumed with the awesomeness of the assignment that even the provision seemed minor compared to the task.

A little later that same evening, a woman from North Carolina came to me and said, "God has spoken to me about you, and He is going to send you on an assignment. It's something so dangerous that legions of angels will be sent with you. He told me to begin to start praying several hours every day for you." I said, "He has?"

Later that evening, the Lord quickened to me the prophecy that I had been given. The Lord said, "I told you the assignment would be given. I have errands for you to do. You will go at my command and I will finance it. It will not be financed in the natural. It will not be financed in any usual way. I will finance it."

By the next morning, the money was in my hand and everything fell in place.

When you give, realize that you are not to put yourself in the limitations of your salary. You are not to put yourself in the limitations of your circumstances. You do not know but that you are seeding toward *your* future assignments in God.

God wants us to live in a different realm. He does not want us to be locked into the natural realm. He wants us to know that giving is a many, many, many faceted thing. You don't give just because you might get a raise, or because someone might come and give you a financial blessing.

Everything that you do has to do with your work in the Kingdom. There are no needs outside of what He needs for you to have or to do. That is why "name it and claim it" was never good to begin with, because it also brings heartbreak and disaster.

As you give to the Lord, you don't know what eternal things are involved. Amounts mean nothing. Obedience is everything!

REAPING THE ONE HUNDRED FOLD RETURN

Matthew 19:29
"And every one that hath forsaken houses, or brethren, or sisters, or father, or mother, or wife, or children, or lands, for my name's sake, shall receive an hundredfold, and shall inherit everlasting life."

If you will serve God and His purposes, He has promised you a one hundred fold return. He has promised it in this life.

We must begin to say serving God is easy. There will be difficulties, but our attitude about the situation has to be an attitude of ease. With ease we will go through the trials and reap the blessings the Lord has ordained for us.

MIRACLES OF OBEDIENCE

Just about everything that has ever happened to Kenneth Hagin has been duplicated in my life. The following is one of the few things that had not happened to me until recently.

The Lord once told Kenneth Hagin to give a month's salary to a minister who had come to his church, who, Kenneth Hagin felt, wasn't a very capable minister.

The Lord had instructed Brother Hagin to let the man minister, and the man didn't even know how to minister. His ministry ability was so poor that Kenneth Hagin wanted to get up and stop him. It was at that point that the Lord told him to give the man a month's salary, to which Kenneth Hagin responded, "A month's salary for that?" He wrestled through the entire service with the idea of giving a month's salary to this minister. But in the end, he did give the man his month's salary.

After that, there were several notable miracles in Brother Hagin's ministry -- people came out of insane asylums whole, and many were delivered from mental disorders. These miracles came because of his obedience. What happened to me recently also happened in connection with obedience.

The things of God somehow always involve a sacrifice. I always pray about my giving, but at a service one night, the Lord impressed me to give much more than I had originally intended. I had a sense in my spirit that something tremendous was going to happen and that it had to do with the offering. I obeyed the Lord and gave what He said to give. That was in the beginning of the service.

At the end of the service, there was a very unusual ministry of the laying on of hands on hands. There was no laying hands on heads -- only laying hands on hands. The laying on of hands went from the tip of the fingers and up the arm. The moment that hands were laid upon me, the most unusual anointing I have ever received came into my hands and through my entire being. I was caught up in the spirit, and the Lord said to me, "You have had special miracles happen from your hands, but from tonight on, very special and extraordinary miracles will take place from your hands."

When I got up off the floor, I didn't go back and enter in the service. I went to a seat in the back and sat down where it was quiet. I felt something unusual happening to my hands. As I looked down, I saw oil coming out of my hands. I had never had that happen before -- it was the first time. It came as droplets, as perspiration would come on your skin, and then my hands began to burn.

We didn't get home until after midnight, and when I looked at my hands, they were like coals of fire and wet with oil. I went to bed, and I pondered the events of the evening in my mind and heart.

At noon the next day, we went out to lunch with several people, and then headed back for the afternoon service. We didn't get back until about ten minutes after the service had begun. All of a sudden, I was informed I was to minister. I didn't even have my Bible, so I had to rush back to where I was staying to get it. Talk about being instant in season and out of season!

As I was delivering the message, the Lord impressed me to tell the people that I had received oil in my hands. The Lord told me that as I laid hands on people, not only would there be miracles of healing and deliverance, but there would be special miracles in which I would take mangled bodies and literally straighten them out -- like you might take a coathanger and straighten it out. The Lord also told me that as I laid my hands on people, if there were mental problems, or any kind of deterioration of the body that had any connection with brain damage, that those things would also be healed.

When it came time to minister to the people, there was a tremendous anointing. There were several hundred people, and many miracles took place. One woman came with a huge tumor under her arm. She told the Lord that she was coming to this meeting, and that she was believing Him to heal her. That tumor was dissolved before everyone's eyes. Many other lumps and tumors also left bodies that afternoon.

A young woman from the Caribbean Islands came up to me the next night. She told me she had been born without a bone in her hip, and that one leg was shorter than the other. She said she had been in pain since birth, but when I laid my hands on her, God put the bone in her leg and now she was perfectly normal. She danced for hours! Many people came and testified of bones and missing organs having been put into their bodies.

I was also asked to pray for a person with Parkinson's disease. The Lord said to tell the person about the anointing I had received, and to tell her, "This will pass" -- that the power of God would go through her until she was completely whole.

In I John, we read that we have an anointing within us, and that the anointing teaches us. Not only does the Holy Spirit teach us, but the anointing also teaches us. As I laid hands on the person with the Parkinson's disease, the anointing was teaching me in the laying on of hands. The Lord said to take my hands and put them all over the woman's jacket. The moment I began to put my hands on the back of her jacket, an incredible surge of power came. It felt like a lightning bolt, and it went through her back and completely healed the area of her back that had deteriorated. I told her to lay the jacket on her pillow and to sleep on it every night.

She called the next morning with the most incredible report that all trembling had stopped in her body. She said that she didn't want to get out of bed because of what she had experienced as she slept on the jacket -- she didn't want to leave that jacket for a second. Remember -- the word was that the power of God would go through her until the healing was completed, and she said that power and power and power was permeating her entire body.

The last night of the series of meetings -- at the time of the offering -- the Lord asked me, "If you could buy what happened to you this weekend, how much do you think it would be worth?" I said, "There's no price for it and I can't buy it." That was a test for me. It was not a test about what I was going to put in the offering. It was God letting me know what was in my own heart.

The power of God and the anointing cannot be bought. Simon the sorcerer tried to buy the power of the Holy Ghost, because he saw that when Peter laid his hands on people, they got the Holy Ghost. When Simon tried to buy it, Peter's response was that Simon was in the gall of bitterness -- that he was cursed. But, through our obedience, all things will be given to us, for the glory of God.

I DO NOT WANT!

Psalm 23

1 *The Lord is my shepherd; I shall not want.*
2 *He maketh me to lie down in green pastures; he leadeth me beside the still waters.*
3 *He restoreth my soul: he leadeth me in the paths of righteousness for his name's sake.*
4 *Yea, though I walk through the valley of the shadow of death, I will fear no evil: for thou art with me; thy rod and thy staff they comfort me.*
5 *Thou preparest a table before me in the presence of mine enemies: thou anointest my head with oil; my cup runneth over.*
6 *Surely goodness and mercy shall follow me all the days of my life: and I will dwell in the house of the Lord for ever.*

The Lord spoke to me and said that we must believe that we do not want -- that we live not wanting. This is the greatest realm of living in prosperity.

"I do not want" means that I have reached a place of divine satisfaction with God. That place of prosperity in the spirit and in the soul must be a place where we reach a full satisfaction in God. That is true prosperity. When we are thoroughly satisfied we don't want anything, because the person who is satisfied in God is one whom God satisfies with all good things.

The Lord is our shepherd. As we receive the Lord, and believe and accept Him as our shepherd, and are satisfied in Him -- not in anything else -- then we are never, ever going to be in want again. The person who is satisfied in God has next to no personal prayer requests. I know this is true -- I rarely have one. Even when a need exists, the satisfaction that comes through the relationship with the Lord somehow pushes the need away and opens the door for the need to be met. This is most assuredly true in the area of financial blessing.

Our group, which meets in Washington, has wonderful and outstanding testimonies of unusual things that have happened in the area of finances. The Lord gave us a prophetic word that He would give unusual compensation to people, and we have seen people compensated in most unusual ways.

God wants us to look to this place of satisfaction -- the place in which you are satisfied with the Lord. Not with yourself, but with the Lord. This always brings in a miraculous provision. You're so happy you don't care what happens. It's not a careless attitude -- it's a satisfied feeling. This is what David is speaking about when he says the Lord is my shepherd, I shall not want.

Imagine that you're a sheep and you're out in this marvelous green pasture. Picture the biggest park you can think of, or an enormous golf green. As a hungry sheep, could you eat all the grass that you see? It would be too much, wouldn't it?

This is what verse 2 is talking about. It is telling us about a provision as far as the eye can see! The one who lies down in green pastures knows that when he wakes up, there is plenty more where the last supply came from! He couldn't possibly finish it all off in one or two feedings. He's got a lifetime to cover all of those pastures, and he's going to be led by the still waters.

The still waters speak about the spirit and the soul that isn't nervous, anxious and worried as to how the provision is going to come. This is the leading of the Lord. But it's up to the sheep to follow the leading, and to follow the Lord into that place where there are still and refreshing waters.

The Lord wants you to proclaim, "I do not want. The Lord is my shepherd. I do not want because He leads me to green pastures." This means He is leading you into financial provision. He's not telling you to stand still and have it dropped in your lap. He is leading you to the pastures of plenty beside the still water where your heart and soul are anchored in His provision.

WINDOWS OF HEAVEN

Of all the things we can give to the Lord, there is nothing that can replace the giving of thanks. No matter what else we might give to Him, it is the fruit of the lips and the giving of thanks that is the greatest thing that we can possibly give.

We read in Malachi 3:10, "Bring ye all the tithes into the storehouse, that there may be meat in mine house, and prove me now herewith, saith the Lord of hosts, if I will not open you the windows of heaven, and pour you out a blessing, that there shall not be room enough to receive it."

The Lord spoke to me about this verse, and I believe it has to do with praise -- not finances. It has to do with the heart and not the pocketbook, even though the pocketbook might be connected to the heart.

In Malachi 3:10, the Lord is speaking about the pouring out of the blessing that there is not room to contain. I don't know of anyone who has ever gotten that blessing. I know some people who have gotten close to it because of the extremity of their need and the awesomeness of the supernatural provision of God, but I don't think any of us have ever truly experienced the blessing that we're not able to contain.

In the Book of Malachi, we find that the nation of Israel was suffering because they were ungrateful and had not recognized the blessings and the provision of God. It didn't have anything to do with finances. It had to do with complaining, instead of pouring out thanksgiving from a grateful heart.

The Lord says that He will open the windows of heaven and pour out. I believe that pouring out has to do with what we pour out from our hearts. When we pour out from our hearts, God then pours out from His heart the abundance of heaven on our behalf.

MEN SHALL GIVE UNTO YOU

It seems that the only time we think about giving is when it's just about the time to do it. If we would begin to allow prosperity to come into our soul all during the week and then give, we would see a marked difference in all of our benefits.

A woman who attends our meetings in Washington had someone follow her out of their office at the conclusion of an appointment one day. This person told her, "I want to seed into your ministry." She said, "I don't have a ministry." Shame on her! Ministry is fulfilling the purposes of God. You can be going to one hundred nations or working locally. Again they said, "I want to give to your ministry." The reply was, "But I don't do anything. I just do whatever the Lord tells me to do." Well, isn't that ministry? This woman was shocked that someone came after her to give to her ministry.

The Word of God teaches us, "Give and it shall be given unto you; good measure, pressed down, and shaken together, and running over." Who is going to do the giving? "... Shall *men* give into your bosom" (Luke 6:38).

We should be so prosperous in our soul that we are open for the unexpected blessing to come. Even people to whom we have gone to pay for a service can turn around and bless us, because the Lord can speak to them and they can give unto us.

"Bless the Lord, oh my soul: and all that is within me, bless his holy name. Bless the Lord, O my soul, and forget not all his benefits." (Psalm 103:1,2) Believe for men to give unto you. This is a benefit. Not only is it a benefit for us, but it's a greater benefit to extend beyond us to be of help to other people.

God doesn't need our money, does He? He doesn't need our sacrifices. We need to give to Him, because that opens the door for the greater blessings to come to us -- that the Lord may be the one who blesses throughout the earth.

VALUE FOR VALUE

In Romans 15:28, Paul is referring to taking an offering when he says, "When therefore I have performed this, and have sealed to them this fruit, I will come by you into Spain." I had read this verse many times, but as I began to read about the meaning of the sealing of the offering, it took on a whole new significance for me.

Spiritually we are to give value for value. The world wants a deal. The world is looking for a bargain. In our house we say, "Faith without good deals is dead."

When I was ministering in Russia several years ago, our interpreter one Sunday morning was a young lady who had studied English, but had never spoken it. When the scripture "Faith without good works is dead" was read, she translated it "Faith without good deals is dead."

We come from a society that prides itself on counterfeits -- everything from counterfeit Gucci watches to fake diamonds and look alike Mercedes. Times are such that one can hardly tell the counterfeits from the originals. We are easily led to believe that counterfeits are the same as and as good as the originals.

Paul spoke about the offering being sealed, the meaning being that the givers sealed unto themselves the content of the spiritual blessing as they gave. They in turn received value for value as they had given, just as we do to this day.

WATER FROM WITHIN

The Word of God says in Matthew 5:6, "Blessed are they which do hunger and thirst after righteousness: for they shall be filled." We should hunger and thirst after the things of God.

In John 4:14 Jesus tells us, "But whosoever drinketh of the water that I shall give him shall never thirst; but the water that I shall give him shall be in him a well of water springing up into everlasting life." This thirst is a state of dryness. The Lord has made a provision that we might never have to experience dryness again. We don't ever have to be dry, because spiritually, we can be like a river in a desert.

That's a glorious provision -- that in the midst of anything, we are never ever going to be dry! The situation around us may be dry and barren, but we shall never thirst, for those that are fed from that spring of living water are fed from the inside, rather than the thirsty man who has to take from the outside. We are fed and watered from within.

Isaiah 44:3,4

3 *For I will pour water upon him that is thirsty, and floods upon the dry ground: I will pour my spirit upon thy seed, and my blessing upon thine offspring;*

4 *And they shall spring up as among the grass, as willows by the water courses.*

Grass is the symbol of people in the scripture. Wherever you read about grass, it always refers to people. Verse four tells us we are not going to be grass people -- we're going to be like the willows. This is the comparison -- that when God begins to put His anointing upon you, you shall spring up among the grass as willows by the water. Instead of being grass people, you're going to be tree people.

The Bible says the grass comes up, it flowers, it looks great, and then the sun comes out and it all burns up and is gone in a day. That's the way most people are -- they're just grass people. But God says He is going to pour water upon the thirsty -- floods upon dry ground -- and He will pour His spirit upon our seed. This means even the seed for the offerings as well as our own physical seed. The Lord is going to pour His spirit upon our seed and His blessing upon our offspring. This means He is even going to bless your offering seed, and your seed is going to have offspring – it is going to produce!

The offspring springs up not like the grass people, but like trees planted by the waters. Trees can take a lot more extremes in weather than grass can. In fact, grass is seasonal -- here today and gone tomorrow. But trees can live a long time by the water.

THE WAY OF THE PEARL

Matthew 13:34, 35

34 *All these things spake Jesus unto the multitude in parables; and without a parable spake he not unto them:*

35 *that it might be fulfilled which was spoken by the prophet, saying I will open my mouth in parables; and I will utter things which have been kept secret from the foundation of the world.*

There are hidden treasures and secret things hidden in the heart that are going to be brought to light and released by the Holy Ghost.

Matthew 13:45, 46

45 *Again, the kingdom of heaven is like unto a merchant man, seeking goodly pearls:*

46 *Who, when he had found one pearl of great price, went and sold all that he had, and bought it.*

The Lord showed me the way of the pearl. Do you know what a pearl is? It's a little piece of sand. Did you ever get sand in your eye? It's the way of the pearl. Around that piece of sand a pearl begins to develop within the oyster, and it comes forth a beautiful jewel.

Many jewels are mentioned in the Bible, but the gates of heaven are of pearl. Diamonds are not on that gate, and there are no rubies or emeralds on it -- the gates are of pearl.

The way to the gate of heaven is the way of the pearl, and it is not an easy way. It is a way in which you are closed in. You are locked in – you are confined. You are even in prison until the day of your coming out and displaying before the earth.

I pray that we may also be brought forth as pearls of great price. May we know the true pearls of great price and not cast our finances before swine. We talk about the hundred fold return, but in order to reap that hundred fold return we must plant and sow in a hundred fold ministry. Your return is determined by the ground in which you sow.

Let us purpose in our hearts to know the true pearls of great price and to give unto true pearls.

EXCHANGE OF POWER

Giving brings a release. Do you know what it means to be released from, and to have things released to you? So many of us have lived in bondage so long that we just want to be loosed and released *from*, but God wants us to begin to think of the releases that are coming *to* us.

God's Word speaks about a law of His spirit that He, Himself, calls the law of release. It is found in Deuteronomy 15:1-6:

1 *At the end of every seven years thou shalt make a release.*
2 *And this is the manner of the release: Every creditor that lendeth ought unto his neighbour shall release it; he shall not exact it of his neighbour, or of his brother; because it is called the Lord's release.*
3 *Of a foreigner thou mayest exact it again: but that which is thine with thy brother thine hand shall release;*
4 *Save when there shall be no poor among you; for the Lord shall greatly bless thee in the land which the Lord thy God giveth thee for an inheritance to possess it:*
5 *Only if thou carefully hearken unto the voice of the Lord thy God, to observe to do all these commandments which I command thee this day.*

6 *For the Lord thy God blesseth thee, as he promised thee: and thou shalt lend unto many nations, but thou shalt not borrow; and thou shalt reign over many nations, but they shall not reign over thee.*

God speaks about a release. Three things are contained in the law of release: forgiving, thanksgiving and giving. Let us examine our hearts in these three areas.

Forgiving means not only forgiving all who have wronged us, but all that have wronged us in any area that involves money. There is hardly a person alive who has not been stolen from financially. There is hardly a person who hasn't had someone -- even a Christian -- do something wrong to them. It is sad to hear Christian businessmen say, "I don't ever want to do business with a Christian again." It is a shame that this is commonly heard.

God demands that you release individuals who have withheld what is rightfully yours in the area of finance. It is the law of release. By the help of the Holy Ghost, just let it go.

The word *lend* in the Bible always means *give*. It is unfortunate that our English translations use the word *lend*, because when we say *lend*, we expect it back. If you will open Vine's Expository Dictionary of New Testament Words, you'll find that *lend* means to give without ever expecting to see it again. So the next time you lend, remember the law of release.

Then there is thanksgiving. Do we give thanksgiving unto God, or are we going to wait to receive to give thanks? God says that when the saints are blessed and when the church gives, it causes abundant thanksgiving to go up to the throne of God, which is well pleasing in His sight.

Then there is giving. The Holy Ghost isn't going to put you into debt or tell you to give some wild amount that is unreasonable for you. The Holy Ghost knows all things about you, and we must obey the Holy Ghost.

God wants to release many things to us -- not just finances. Jesus said, "If therefore you have not been faithful in the unrighteous mammon, who will commit to your trust the true riches?" There is a relationship between your pocketbook and your miracle ministry. There is a relationship between money and miracles. Money is the greatest vehicle of exchange in the world, and miracles are the greatest vehicle of exchange and power in the kingdom of God.

THE POWER OF THE ENDLESS BLESSING

There seems to be a great deal of misunderstanding concerning the area that we call *tithes*. Countless people have come to me with the question: Where do I pay my tithes? It seems that many people are confused as to where their tithe should go.

First of all, I have to say that the tithe is not a major issue in the New Testament. The word *tithe* means a tenth. Therefore the giving of a tithe means the giving of a tenth -- ten percent of something.

In the Old Testament it was not only money that was tithed, it was ten percent of everything that one possessed. Tithing went far beyond the giving of money -- it involved every single area in which one had *possession*. That's why Jesus spoke to the Pharisees and said, "Woe unto you scribes and Pharisees, hypocrites! for ye pay tithe of mint and anise and cummin, and have omitted the weightier matters of the law, judgment, mercy, and faith: these ought ye to have done, and not to leave the other undone" (Matthew 23:23).

Hosea 4:6

6 *My people are destroyed for lack of knowledge: because thou hast rejected knowledge, I will also reject thee, that thou shalt be no priest to me:*

seeing thou hast forgotten the law of thy God, I will also forget thy children.

The church at large has little comprehension of the major spiritual concepts of the New Testament. There seems to be only a slight understanding of the many faceted areas of giving, receiving and financial recovery. In fact, most of the time the church is living under the Old Testament law. For this reason, there is much confusion in the church about the giving of the tithes, and to whom the tithes are to go.

Most people in the church today consider the bulk of their giving to be the tithe, and the offering to be minor. However, the offering is not governed by any limitation or percentage. Nowhere is it written that the offering cannot be far more than the tithe! The tithe only means ten percent. Even though someone may say they are tithing twenty percent, the word *tithe* itself means ten percent. *Offering* means whatever you, of your own free will, want to give.

Malachi 3:10-12

10 *Bring ye all the tithes into the storehouse, that there may be meat in mine house, and prove me now herewith, saith the Lord of hosts, if I will not open you the windows of heaven, and pour you out a blessing, that there shall not be room enough to receive it.*

11 *And I will rebuke the devourer for your sakes, and he shall not destroy the fruits of your ground; neither shall your vine cast her fruit before the time in the field, saith the Lord of hosts.*

12 *And all nations shall call you blessed: for ye shall be a delightsome land, saith the Lord of hosts.*

Notice that verse 10 is not speaking about a tithe -- it's talking about *all* the tithes. It gives instructions to bring in a tenth of *everything*. When tithes and offerings are received, churches frequently quote this scripture.

As we should all know, in the Old Testament only one place -- the temple -- was the storehouse. From the temple *all* needs of the community were met. Not only were the needs of the temple itself and the priests connected with the temple met, but the needs of the poor and the needs of the entire community came from this one place. There was only one place of worship, and that was the temple.

Today we no longer have a temple, for the temple was destroyed after Jesus was raised from the dead. We are told, "know ye not that your body is the temple of the Holy Ghost" (I Corinthians 6:19), but we do attend what we call the local churches. It is commonly taught that the tithe is to go to the local church, and the offering may go elsewhere.

Where Does the Tithe Go?

First I have to ask a question to solve the problem. The problem lies in who receives the tithe. If a tithe or an offering is received, to whom is the tithe given?

In studying the subject of the tithe, we must pay close attention to whom the Bible says should receive the tithe. What does the Bible say about where the tithe goes? The Bible says the tithe is that which is given to the priest. The priest receives the tithe.

In order to understand any subject in the Bible, we must follow a rule of study called the law of first mention, referring to the first time a subject is introduced in scripture. The first time a subject is introduced a framework is established, and a foundation is laid upon which that subject is built. You cannot begin at any other point -- you must find where it was initially introduced.

The giving of the tithe was introduced in the Book of Genesis. Genesis is the seedbed for the entire Bible. There is no subject in the Bible that is not contained in the Book of Genesis. It is all there.

What is mentioned in the Bible first -- offerings or tithes? Offerings are mentioned before tithes. Where is the first place that an offering is mentioned? We find that the offering is first mentioned in Genesis 4.

Genesis 4:3-8

3 *And in process of time it came to pass, that Cain brought of the fruit of the ground an offering unto the Lord.*

4 *And Abel, he also brought of the firstlings of his flock and of the fat thereof. And the Lord had respect unto Abel and to his offering:*

5 *But unto Cain and to his offering he had not respect. And Cain was very wroth, and his countenance fell.*

6 *And the Lord said unto Cain, Why art thou wroth? and why is thy countenance fallen?*

7 *If thou doest well, shalt thou not be accepted? and if thou doest not well, sin lieth at the door. And unto thee shall be his desire, and thou shalt rule over him.*

8 *And Cain talked with Abel his brother: and it came to pass, when they were in the field, that Cain rose up against Abel his brother, and slew him.*

Abel's offering was holy and acceptable unto the Lord. Cain's offering was not acceptable unto the Lord. The subject of the blood sacrifice is also involved here -- Abel made a blood sacrifice and Cain did not. But there is more here than the aspect of the blood sacrifice. Cain gave an offering of his own work, whereas Abel gave an offering from the blessings God gave to him.

God requires and accepts offerings, but he only wants acceptable offerings. He will not accept an offering in which the heart motive is not pure -- it must be holy and acceptable unto the Lord.

In Genesis 14, the word *tithe* is first mentioned after the battle of the kings, in which Abram went out with his 318 servants and recovered all that had been lost.

Genesis 14:18-24

18 *And Melchizedek king of Salem brought forth bread and wine: and he was the priest of the most high God.*

19 *And he blessed him, and said, Blessed be Abram of the most high God, possessor of heaven and earth;*

20 *And blessed be the most high God, which hath delivered thine enemies into thy hand. And he gave him tithes of all.*
21 *And the king of Sodom said unto Abram, Give me the persons, and take the goods to thyself.*
22 *And Abram said to the king of Sodom, I have lift up mine hand unto the Lord, the most high God, the possessor of heaven and earth,*
23 *That I will not take from a thread even to a shoelatchet, and that I will not take any thing that is thine, lest thou shouldest say, I have made Abram rich;*
24 *Save only that which the young men have eaten, and the portion of the men which went with me, Aner, Eshcol, and Mamre, let them take their portion.*

There is something most significant here in Abraham giving the tithe. Abraham paid a tithe to the priest. All tithes *must* be paid to the priest.

The first mention of the word *tithe* in the Bible occurred with Abraham. It was a gesture of his own heart that caused Abraham to pay a tenth of *all*, for no law dictated that he do so. He didn't pay just a tenth of his money -- he paid a tenth of all that he had. To whom did he pay it? He paid it to the priest of the most high God -- Melchizedek, the prince of peace. This speaks about the Lord Himself -- one who had no beginning of days nor end of days, without geneology, totally outside of the law. This in no way involves the Old Testament Mosaic law, but refers to the eternal law of the spirit.

The paying of tithes is ordained by Old Testament law. The New Testament law is different, for it is the law of the spirit of life in Christ Jesus which sets us free from the law of sin and death. These things need to be made clear in the body of Christ. We have a church today that is living, by and large, under Old Testament law, and has never, ever moved into the law of the spirit of the New Testament for which Jesus gave His life.

It is important to see that Abraham didn't pay a tithe to just anybody. He paid a tithe into a mystery of God, and it was a tithe of everything with which God had blessed him. The tithe must be given from that with which God has blessed us. It is not something that we decide to give or do, but it is a returning to the Lord of that which He has given unto us.

Abraham was blessed by Melchizedek, and he received a blessing from this King and Prince of Salem. Abraham was ministered to by Melchizedek, who gave him bread and wine and blessed him. *After he was ministered to and blessed, Abraham then paid the tithe back to Melchizedek.*

The King of Sodom didn't minister to Abraham at all, nor did Abraham receive any blessing from him. He was one of the many Abraham helped. When we read how Abraham recovered all of the people and possessions of those cities, it is understandable that the King of Sodom would be grateful. He said, "Give me the persons, and take the goods to thyself" (Genesis 14:21).

Abraham's response to the King of Sodom was, "I have lift up mine hand unto the Lord, the most high God, the possessor of heaven and earth, That I will not take from a thread even to a shoelatchet, and that I will not take any thing that is thine, lest thou shouldest say, I have made Abram rich: Save only that which the young men have eaten, and the portion of the men which went with me, Aner, Eshcol, and Mamre; let them take their portion" (Genesis 14:22-24). Abraham took nothing for himself from the King of Sodom, for God, Himself, made Abraham rich.

Tithes speak of victory. A tithe is not something that one pays to get out of a mess. I want to make this very clear: Abraham gave back out of the victory! He wasn't paying and giving his way out of debt. He was tithing back of the victory! The Lord wants victory within our hearts. We are to be tithing back because of victories -- not trying to buy our way out of debt. (Many times it will get you out of debt, but that is not how we are to approach it.)

Where battles are fought, victories are gained and spoils are taken. To the victor belong the spoils. There are things to be rendered unto men and things to be rendered unto God, and you had better make sure that all the portions are handled properly.

It was God who prospered Abraham all along, and like Abel, his flocks and everything he had kept increasing. He couldn't increase it himself -- it wasn't his own labor. It was like businesses that just keep multiplying once they get going -- it's not because that person is working ten more hours a day. This is the increase. *The tithe is given from the increase.*

It is important to recognize that the tithe was paid to the priest. Today there is confusion in the church over where the tithe is to be paid. We almost always hear that the tithe should be paid to the local church, and then all other ministries get what's left over. You can hardly go to any church that doesn't tell you that. I'm not telling you what to do -- I'm just telling you what the scripture says. The Bible says that *Abraham paid tithes to Melchizedek,* the Prince of Salem, ***who blessed him. He paid to the one through whom he was blessed.*** He didn't pay to someone who was not blessing him, for ***the lesser gives the blessing to the greater.***

In the New Testament, the only time the tithe is mentioned is in the Book of Hebrews. All teaching concerning the tithe, even in the Book of Hebrews, refers back to Chapter 14 of the Book of Genesis. It is important to ask the Holy Spirit to enlighten the eyes of your understanding to see exactly what the Word of God is communicating to you.

The law of the tithe was established at a point in time before we had what we call the Mosaic law. We also have to realize that Abraham lived before the time of the law. He was outside of the law, just as we are outside of the Mosaic law.

Abraham, by his faithfulness and righteousness which he achieved by faith in the living God, entered into a covenant with God which God cannot disannul. God has a covenant with Abraham, and He has a New Testament covenant with us through Jesus Christ.

The old covenant was fulfilled in Jesus. We are told, "For there is verily a disannulling of the commandment going before for the weakness and unprofitableness thereof. For the law made nothing perfect, but the bringing in of a better hope did; by the which we draw nigh unto God. By so much was Jesus made a surety of a better testament" (Hebrews 7:18, 19, 22).

We are living today under a new covenant with better promises. I believe the Lord wants the church to realize the benefits of these better promises and to possess better understanding, better enlightenment, better anointing -- better everything. Instead, most of the church embraces an Old Testament mentality where the tithe is concerned, yet they believe they are fulfilling a New Testament requirement. With this kind of thinking, most of the church pays little attention to the broader subject of the leadings of the Holy Spirit concerning offerings.

At the same time, in neglecting to understand that tithes are plural, the New Testament believer perceives this act of worship as a fulfillment of an obligation to give ten percent of their paycheck for the week or month, failing to see that the Old Testament believer brought tithes of *everything* into the storehouse. The fact remains that the scripture does not speak about a single tithe -- it says *tithes of all.* The Old Testament, as well as the New Testament, talks about tithes -- the plural form, not about ten percent of your paycheck, but tithes of everything being brought into the storehouse.

In recent years, much emphasis has been placed on receiving the hundred fold return for our giving. The idea of receiving such a blessing thrills our heart, but the means by which such faith becomes operational in the believer often escapes us. In order to become the recipient of the hundred fold return, *we must begin by giving to where the anointing is present and operating.*

It is most important to realize that the field into which one plants determines the amount of the return that will be yielded. Therefore, it only stands to reason that tithes and offerings must be given to a ministry that exhibits a holy and an anointed life. Holiness, dedication to the call, and an anointing should be evidenced in the life and ministry to which one gives. To better understand the true nature of a holy priesthood, let us now look at the office of the priest as the scripture presents it.

We know, as believers in the Lord Jesus Christ living under a better covenant with better promises, that the tithes and offerings must be paid to Jesus. In Genesis 14 we see Jesus prefigured in Melchizedek. Then we read in Psalm 110:1 - 4, "The Lord said unto my Lord, Sit thou at my right hand, until I make thine enemies thy footstool. ... Thou art a priest forever." In the Hebrew it says, *"you have been made a priest forever upon my word."* In other words, it is the Word of God; it is irrevocable and can never be changed. So Jesus is the eternal high priest who has passed into the eternal heaven of heavens. He has entered into the holy of holies once and for all by His blood to purchase our redemption. He is the mediator of the better covenant with better promises.

If the tithe is to be paid to the priest, then we need to know who the priest is. The New Testament tells us that we -- all of us -- have been made kings and priests unto God. So we are all to be in the priesthood, and we are called a royal priesthood, a holy people.

What is a holy people? A people separated from the people of the world. Likewise, the things that pertain to God's people are to be separated unto Him, and it is up to the Lord as to what is done with those things. It is not man's decision.

Abraham is a great example. He gave a tenth of everything to the priest. He did not give to someone who did not minister to him. Abraham was ministered to and blessed by Melchizedek, and to him Abraham paid his tithes.

Only once a year, under the law, did the high priest enter into the holy of holies to make sacrifice, and to bring offerings on behalf of the people. There were many priests in the priesthood, but only the high priest went into the holy of holies once a year to make atonement for the sins of the people. Jesus is our high priest who has forever passed into the heavens to appear before the presence of God on our behalf.

There is only one high priest, and that is Jesus. He is prefigured and foreshadowed on this earth in what we call the fivefold ministry. The fivefold ministry encompasses the major facets of the ministry of Jesus, and is comprised of apostles, prophets, pastors, teachers and evangelists. Just as Jesus is the great gift of God to the world, the Holy Spirit is the gift of God to the believer. Apostles, prophets, pastors, teachers and evangelists are ministry gifts to the body of Christ.

Ephesians 4:9-16

9 *(Now that he ascended, what is it but that he also descended first into the lower parts of the earth?*

10 *He that descended is the same also that ascended up far above all heavens, that he might fill all things.)*

11 *And he gave some, apostles; and some, prophets; and some, evangelists; and some, pastors and teachers.*

12 *For the perfecting of the saints, for the work of the ministry, for the edifying of the body of Christ;*

13 *Till we all come in the unity of the faith, and of the knowledge of the Son of God, unto a perfect man, unto the measure of the stature of the fulness of Christ:*

14 *That we henceforth be no more children, tossed to and fro, and carried about with every wind of doctrine, by the sleight of men, and cunning craftiness, whereby they lie in wait to deceive;*

15 *But speaking the truth in love, may grow up into him in all things, which is the head, even Christ:*

16 *From whom the whole body fitly joined together and compacted by that which every joint supplieth, according to the effectual working in the measure of every part, maketh increase of the body unto the edifying of itself in love.*

Therefore, that which we call the fivefold ministry is really a gift of ministry to the people. In the Old Testament, the people were ministered to by priests and prophets who were the teachers of God's word and will. We are *all* priests and kings under the new covenant, but those who are apostles, prophets, evangelists, pastors and teachers (part of the fivefold ministry) stand in a higher position of ministry than other ministries within the body of Christ. God has given them an anointing that will bring about this perfection, or building up of the body of Christ, so that the whole body of Christ may stand in the stature of the fulness of the maturity of Jesus Christ. So how can tithes and offerings come only to the pastor, when the rest of those in the fivefold ministry are of equal importance?

Where is the New Testament Storehouse?

For most people, it is the local church. However, the church is universal in scope, and the local church is but one aspect of the universal church. Tithes must come to ***the*** church. There is ***one*** church. There is one faith. There is one baptism. There is one Holy Spirit. There is only one way to give, and that is by the spirit, by faith, under the direction of the Holy Spirit, who is leading and guiding the church. Therefore, it is difficult to understand why the idea prevails that the tithe must only be given to one segment of the church. To hold an opinion like that excludes the other aspects of priesthood.

We don't ever find the apostles saying they received a tithe. We do hear them saying that they received offerings. We also hear Paul saying that many times people gave sacrificially for certain missionary journeys or for the poor, and that their giving was holy and acceptable unto the Lord. However, the word *tithe* is never used when these examples of giving are related.

Today, people seem to be very confused. They might have a leading of the Holy Spirit to give to a particular person or ministry, but are told they may not. There is nothing written in the New Testament that says the tithe must be brought only to one place. Everything that one does must be under the direction of the Holy Spirit.

There are many people who go to churches where things are not right. I cannot tell you the number of spirit-filled people I've spoken with over the years who go to churches where there are unsaved ministers. These people have given their tithes to these churches where the ministers aren't even saved because they believe they are doing the right thing. But they are deceived. Then there are people in churches that God never called them to, in places that are not right before God. They are blessing something that is not blessing them -- neither is it blessed by God. They are really heaping a judgment on themselves because they are doing things that are not according to God's laws or spirit.

Even though the Old Testament is a type and shadow, it puts forth the understanding and the meaning of different spiritual areas that we need to understand. The type and shadow must be fulfilled, and all types and shadows are fulfilled in Jesus. Therefore, today we do not have dozens of kinds of offerings to make up for all of the things we did wrong during the week. We are living under a better covenant with a better promise. Jesus is taking care of all offering through Him, for Him, to Him, and by Him, via the gifts that He, Himself, has placed in the body of Christ. I see no place in the scripture where it is stated that the tithe goes to the pastor, but may not go to the apostle -- or where the tithe goes to the pastor, but not the prophet -- or where the tithe goes to the pastor and not to the teacher -- or where the tithe goes to the pastor and not to the evangelist. *The tithe is to go wherever the Holy Spirit sends it.*

New Testament Order

If we are in a local church that is helping us to become strong in the Lord, and is bringing all aspects of ministry to us, by all means the tithe must go there, for the tithe is then coming into the fulness of the ministry gifts that Jesus has placed in the body of Christ. Something is wrong with a local church that is not feeding its people or bringing all aspects of ministry to its people, yet says the tithe cannot be given elsewhere. That is outside of the order of the New Testament.

In the Old Testament, ministerial services came through the Levitical priesthood. When the New Testament came into effect -- when Jesus rose from the dead and the day of Pentecost arrived -- the Holy Spirit was poured out upon the church and a new form of worship was instituted. Worshippers were born who would now worship the Father in spirit and in truth.

Deuteronomy 33:8

8 *And of Levi he said, Let thy Thummim and thy Urim be with thy holy one, whom thou didst prove at Massah, and with whom thou didst strive at the waters of Meribah;*

What is the thummim and the urim? They are two Hebrew words: thummim means perfection and urim means lights. The priest was the only one who could call upon the urim and the thummim. The thummim and urim was a means by which the will of God could be known in a situation. When David was preparing for battle he would go to the priest, who had the urim and thummim, and enquire as to whether or not he should go. Responses to these enquiries were not simply yes or no. Many times quite lengthy answers were given, along with specific instructions from the Lord.

The priest was the only one who had this divine connection with the will of God. The ordinary person did not have this personal connection with God, to know His will. *Everyone* had to go to the priest to get the divine will and counsel of God for a situation. This was part of the blessing that went along with the priesthood.

The urim and the thummim are fulfilled in Jesus Christ, for He is the way, the truth and the life. He always points the way. He is the prophet, the bishop of our souls, and He always has the final word on all things.

As believers in Jesus under the new covenant, we can know the will of God for ourselves at all times. Romans 8:14 tells us, "For as many as are led by the Spirit of God, they are the sons of God." Hebrews 8:11 says, "And they shall not teach every man his neighbour, and every man his brother, saying, Know the Lord: for all shall know me, from the least to the greatest."

Every one of us can know the will of God, and every one of us can get the answer for ourselves. We are not to run to the prophets and the priests to find out what the will of God is, although many are doing just that -- running, running, running -- trying to find out what the Lord has to say through another person. God will use another person, but that is not how the New Testament believer is to hear from the Lord. The New Testament believer is to be led by the spirit of God. If you cannot hear from God yourself and you have to keep running to a prophet, there is something wrong in your relationship with the Lord.

The priest is called the holy one because he has separated himself. The priest is one who knows the will of God, and one who has separated himself for the purposes of priesthood. He has to live differently than the people. It doesn't mean that what the people do is wrong, but he must live differently by virtue of the fact that he is called to the priesthood. His life, in every respect, has to be different, and he, as a minister of the gospel, must have a different lifestyle from the rest of the people in his church or ministry. He may not be allowed to do things that the congregation may be permitted to do for reasons that might only be known to God.

Deuteronomy 33:9

9 *Who said unto his father and to his mother, I have not seen him; neither did he acknowledge his brethren, nor knew his own children: for they have observed thy word, and kept thy covenant.*

A true priest, or minister, can never, ever put his family above his ministry. His mother, his father, or his children, cannot hold a place in his heart above the Lord or the will of God. When it involves the work of the ministry, the true minister must show himself to be impartial to his family. As Jesus said, "He that loveth father or mother more than me is not worthy of me: and he that loveth son or daughter more than me is not worthy of me" (Matthew 10:37).

It is important to understand that following the Lord wholly and delighting to be obedient to His will will never cause a mother, a father, a husband, a wife, or children to suffer. In fact, the greater blessing for all will prevail when God's divine order in the ministry is established. This is one of the main reasons Abraham was chosen by God.

We always think of Abraham chosen as a man of faith, and of course that's what he was. But God chose Abraham from among men because God was first in Abraham's life, and everyone else came second. Abraham also instilled this order into his family: "And the Lord said, Shall I hide from Abraham that thing which I do; For I know him, that he will command his children and his household after him, and they shall keep the way of the Lord, to do justice and judgment; that the Lord may bring upon Abraham that which he hath spoken of him" (Genesis 18:17, 19).

Deuteronomy 33:10

10 *They shall teach Jacob thy judgments, and Israel thy law: they shall put incense before thee, and whole burnt sacrifice upon thine altar.*

Priests had an anointing and an ability to communicate the true laws of God and the true judgments of the people. They were fully functional in the anointing of the priesthood.

Incense was only used in the holy of holies, and only the high priest entered the holy of holies. Incense always speaks about prayers that go up to the throne of God. In the Book of Revelation, we read about the odor and the incense of the prayers. The odor and the incense always goes up.

It is interesting that the word *offering* itself means *to go up.* It doesn't mean to give out -- it means something that goes up. Everything connected with tithes and offerings holds the meaning of *going up* -- that which actually goes up and ascends into the presence of God.

The priest was the only one who could pray for the people, because he went in before the presence of the Lord and offered the incense that went up and was received in the presence of God. A true priest is one whose prayers go up.

Deuteronomy 33:11

11 *Bless, Lord, his substance, and accept the work of his hands: smite through the loins of them that rise against him, and of them that hate him, that they rise not again.*

This verse is talking about the blessing of the Lord for the priest. The priest has paid a higher and a dearer price: their whole life is totally devoted to the Lord, with family and personal interests also consecrated unto the Lord.

The priest -- Old Testament as well as New Testament -- has to come before the Lord to pray for all people. God so loved *the world* that He gave His only begotten Son. The duty of the priest is to represent everyone.

Priesthood is not attained because you want it. It is given to you because it is ordained by God for you to be a priest. When it is ordained for you to be a priest, (or in the case of the fivefold ministry, if it is ordained for you to be in that position), it means that you have to accept the responsibility and care for every person who places themselves under your ministry.

In the local church, there must also be a taking care when it comes to the offering. There are plenty of people who don't have any money and want the local church to take care of them, but it must be a legitimate need. It should be a need of someone connected with that particular body of believers, and not some floating need that wants to float right out the door with the offering in hand.

Verse 11 of Deuteronomy 33 also tells us that God will stand with the ministry against anybody who is out to destroy the ministry, or seeking to stand against the anointing of God.

The Bible has much to say about the blessing of the double portion that comes to the firstborn -- mainly to the firstborn of the priest. Most of us have prayed at one time or another for the double portion of God's spirit. We need to be aware that the receiving of the double portion promised to the firstborn involves assuming a double responsibility and double care. It means that you take much more upon yourself -- many more people, many more needs, much more care.

In the Old Testament, the priest was a mediator between God and man, but now Jesus is the only mediator between God and man. Today, the whole priesthood has been fulfilled in Jesus, even though we have individual ministers within the body of Christ who fulfill certain types and shadows.

The priest makes the offering and represents the people in their offering. "For every high priest taken from among men is ordained for men in things pertaining to God, that he may offer both gifts and sacrifices for sins" (Hebrews 5:1). Therefore, he has a great responsibility.

He who receives the tithes and offerings represents the people who give to that ministry. He represents them before God, and he is responsible before God for the use of those tithes and offerings. He is also responsible to exercise his faith for the people in

regard to their financial offerings, that they might truly receive the blessings promised the giver.

The minister is going to be given a double blessing for his service, but if he is not a good steward of God's finances, or if his heart is not right, he will receive the double judgment.

A minister must be one who is truly helping the people to progress spiritually. He must have an ability to clearly teach and communicate the things that pertain to God. His involvement with and the teaching of things that pertain to this life, and the wisdom of this world, must be secondary to ministering the true riches of the gospel.

Hebrews 5:2-4

2 Who can have compassion on the ignorant, and on them that are out of the way; for that he himself also is compassed with infirmity.

3 And by reason hereof he ought, as for the people, so also for himself, to offer for sins.

4 But no man taketh this honour unto himself, but he that is called of God, as was Aaron.

We cannot call ourselves into the fivefold ministry. We must be called by God in the same way that Aaron was called, and the same way that each person in the Bible was called. *We also must be called.* There is no such thing as choosing our position or placement in the kingdom of God. ***All placement in the church is by God, and not by church board or committee!***

Hebrews 5:5, 6

5 *So also Christ glorified not himself to be made an high priest; but he that said unto him, Thou art my Son, today have I begotten thee.*

6 *As he saith also in another place, Thou art a priest for ever after the order of Melchizedek.*

The scripture says that Melchizedek neither had beginning of days nor end of days, so it's speaking about Jesus. The reference is that this Melchizedek is a type and a shadow because there is no mention of his family in the Bible. He probably lived and was an actual person, but there is no mention of a family. We don't know anything about him, which is unusual, because the Old Testament links everyone to family. You were your family, good or bad. But there is no geneology for Melchizedek, and not even a reference to a family can be found. This is the kind of priest Jesus is -- no family, no beginning, no end -- eternal.

Hebrews 5:7, 8

7 *Who in the days of his flesh, when he had offered up prayers and supplications with strong crying and tears unto him that was able to save him from death, and was heard in that he feared;*

8 *Though he were a Son, yet learned he obedience by the things which he suffered;*

Hebrews 7:1-7

1 *For this Melchizedek, king of Salem, priest of the most high God, who met Abraham returning from the slaughter of the kings and blessed him;*

2 *To whom also Abraham gave a tenth part of all; first being by interpretation King of righteousness,* *and after that also King of Salem, which is, King of peace;*

3 *Without father, without mother, without descent, having neither beginning of days, nor end of life; but made like unto the Son of God; abideth a priest continually.*

4 *Now consider how great this man was, unto whom even the patriarch Abraham gave the tenth of the spoils.*

5 *And verily they that are of the sons of Levi, who receive the office of the priesthood, have a commandment to take tithes of the people according to the law, that is, of their brethren, though they come out of the loins of Abraham:*

6 *But he whose descent is not counted from them received tithes of Abraham, and blessed him that had the promises.*

7 *And without all contradiction the less is blessed of the better.*

Now I'm going to say something that is very touchy. There are many people who have gone to ministries for years and have actually achieved a far greater spiritual stature than the ministry they attend. There is something unseemly and out of order about that, because the lesser is not ordained to bless the greater. The greater should bless the lesser. You don't send a genius to kindergarten; likewise, you should not keep supporting something that you have thoroughly outgrown and which is no longer able to edify you further. There are far too many people supporting ministries that do not cause them to spiritually grow and mature. The end result is spiritual hunger and thirst, and complete dissatisfaction.

People are afraid to do the wrong thing, so they keep doing the same thing, even though it doesn't make any sense. Some have wrong reasons for continuing in the same path. What are the motives of the heart? Why are we doing the things we are doing? We have to take a look at the reasons. Are they reasons that are holy and acceptable unto God, or are they reasons that man accepts? Are they man's traditional beliefs, or are they really what the Word of God says?

Hebrews 7:8, 9

8 *And here men that die receive tithes; but there he receiveth them, of whom it is witnessed that he liveth.*

9 *And as I may so say, Levi, also, who receiveth tithes, payeth tithes in Abraham.*

Levi paid tithes to Abraham before he was even born. The unborn were paying tithes through Abraham, and received the blessings, because Abraham was paying his tithes the right way, in the right place, and with the right motive, and he brought those blessings to his descendants. Therefore as parents, we need to know that there is an *unseen principle and law working behind the scenes:* that what we are sowing today, we are also reaping for our children in the future.

Hebrews 7:10-12

10 *For he was yet in the loins of his father, when Melchizedek met him.*

11 *If therefore perfection were by the Levitical priesthood, (for under it the people received the law,) what further need was there that another* *priest should rise after the order of Melchizedek, and not be called after the order of Aaron?*

12 *For the priesthood being changed, there is made of necessity a change also of the law.*

A new covenant came into operation, and a new priesthood came into being. Therefore, the rules that governed the old priesthood ceased, and new rules came in along with the new priesthood. Now there is one high priest. There are ministers before the Lord and before the people who have a responsibility before God, but only one high priest, only one head -- Jesus.

There are new rules now -- we no longer have the law. We have what is called the law of the spirit of life in Christ Jesus. We have a law that is now written in our hearts. This is the new covenant.

Hebrews 8:8-10

8 *For finding fault with them, he saith, Behold, the days come, saith the Lord, when I will make a new covenant with the house of Israel and with the house of Judah:*

9 *Not according to the covenant that I made with their fathers in the day when I took them by the hand to lead them out of the land of Egypt; because they continued not in my covenant, and I regarded them not, saith the Lord.*

10 *For this is the covenant that I will make with the house of Israel after those days, saith the Lord; I will put my laws into their mind, and write them in their hearts: and I will be to them a God, and they shall be to me a people;*

This unwritten law in our hearts is going to speak to us, and we've got to be in touch with the Holy Spirit speaking to our hearts. This is the new law and the new priesthood. As New Testament believers, we are going to have to know what the Lord says to us -- not what all these surveys and groups of people have to say about what, where, how, and to whom things go.

That which was the storehouse in the Old Testament is *not* the storehouse in the New Testament. We must know what is stored within each individual ministry to be able to ascertain what kind of provision can even come forth from the New Testament storehouses. It is not the same as it was in the Old Testament.

Hebrews 7:13-16

13 *For he of whom these things are spoken pertaineth to another tribe, of which no man gave attendance at the altar.*

14 *For it is evident that our Lord sprang out of Juda; of which tribe Moses spake nothing concerning priesthood.*

15 *And it is yet far more evident: for that after the similitude of Melchizedek there ariseth another priest,*

16 *Who is made, not after the law of a carnal commandment, but after the power of an endless life.*

This is the law of the new priesthood -- the new priesthood in which Jesus Christ is *the* high priest. We are the under priests of the royal priesthood. Jesus is the one who enters into the throne of God, and comes into the presence of the Father on our behalf. He is the *only* mediator between God and man, and He is the only mediator of the New Testament.

A mediator is not a mediator of one, the scripture says (Galatians 3:20). This means that Jesus is a connector or a go-between -- a bridge that spans the gap between the Old Testament and the New Testament. He connects the two and bridges the gap.

A mediator is one who speaks for and shows the relationship between two sides. Jesus, as the mediator, has fulfilled every single thing in the Old Testament to bring forth the fulness of the New Testament.

The old covenant was good -- the Bible states that the law was good. Every single thing that God ever did was good. There is nothing bad in the law. Those who live by the law can be blessed by the law. We have plenty of non-believers being blessed every day -- some even more than believers -- because they are obeying the law of God, whether they know it or not. There are blessings connected with the law, but there are far greater blessings pertaining to the unlimited inheritance provided for in the New Testament, where grace and truth abound *outside the limitation of the law.*

The law of the Old Testament was under a carnal commandment. Therefore, it had a beginning, an end, and it had limitations. Whenever you need a miracle, you do not want to be under a limitation! Throughout the Old Testament, there were breakthroughs out of the limitation of the law -- foreshadowing and showing a type of Jesus Christ. We must get out of this Old

Testament mode which has been presented to us as the New Testament. There is nothing wrong with the Old Testament – it is good, but there is something so much better!

There are times when all of us need to be delivered from the handwriting of ordinances against us -- under the Old Testament, we could not be delivered outside of a sovereign act of God. Under the New Testament, the sovereign will of God is expressed in the mercy of Jesus Christ that delivers us from the handwriting of ordinances. That is why it is so important that we pass from the ministry of death into the administration of life, and life more abundant.

The Old Testament -- even the law of the tithe and all of the law of the inheritance -- dealt with an earthly fulfillment, and blessings that were tied into the observance of this law, through which you would be blessed. The New Testament gives us an *eternal inheritance* in the heavenlies. Many people, not understanding the eternal inheritance, prefer the temporal one. They think what they need is right now -- the temporal -- not knowing that the eternal blessing of every spiritual blessing and heavenly gift provides for the temporal, as well as establishes us in an eternal inheritance reserved for us in the ages to come.

We don't want only the temporal blessings connected with the commandments. We want to fully experience the power of an endless life, as well as the power of the endless blessing. This is what Abraham was tithing into. He tithed into an endless life -- Jesus. He tithed into something unending in the heavens.

Abraham had a perception beyond the natural understanding of the giving of the tithe. If we persist in the "if I give this, then my business will prosper" thinking, we will fall short of the great and continual blessings that God has in store for us. Abraham was not a victim of that type of thinking. He was farsighted, and tithed into the eternities. Jesus said, "Your father Abraham rejoiced to see my day: and he saw it, and was glad" (John 8:56). Abraham saw far ahead. He didn't see or live for the moment, or only for his generation on the earth -- he lived for the day of Jesus Christ.

The Lord wants us to enter into the power of the endless life which is in Jesus Christ. His desire is for all of us to enter into the power of the endless blessing -- where we are not locked into the law of a carnal commandment with temporal blessings only.

May the eyes of your understanding be enlightened that you may know the hope of His calling, the riches of the glory of His inheritance in the saints, and the exceeding greatness of His power to us who believe (Ephesians 1:18, 19). In the days ahead, as you obey His voice and pay close attention to His leadings, you will truly find the power of the endless blessing to be a reality in your life.